Wildlife

of Grand Teton National Park

Written by

Charles Craighead

Photography by

Henry H. Holdsworth

Official Guidebook

of Grand Teton National Park

Table *of* Contents

Introduction

Famous for its variety of dramatic wildlife species, Grand Teton National Park (GTNP) has long been a destination for photographers, birdwatchers, and wildlife enthusiasts. Dozens of television programs have focused on the park's natural history. Biologists come to conduct research on rare plant and animal species, and many new visitors who travel here to see the Teton Range are as surprised and fascinated with the herds of bison and elk as they are with the mountain scenery. Why here? What makes Jackson Hole and the Tetons abound with wildlife? The animals are protected, of course, but they aren't tame, and there are no fences or barriers to keep them here. Many of them, in fact, leave the park for part of the year.

Two main factors contribute to the numbers and varieties of wildlife. First, homesteaders and farmers ignored the Jackson Hole valley until late in the settlement of the West. It had long, severe winters, limited access, and very little decent farmland. Much better opportunities for agriculture existed over the mountains in Idaho, and land was free. The first homesteaders didn't arrive here until 1884, twelve years after Yellowstone was established as a national park. This late settlement gave the valley time for the rest of the expanding country to realize some of their environmental mistakes, such as the decimation of sixty million bison on the Great Plains and the clear-cutting of miles and miles of invaluable forests. By the time Jackson Hole was settled, a new era of national conservation was underway, game laws were enacted and enforced, and huge areas of land were being set aside. Jackson Hole was in the heart of all this, and its new residents were extremely proud of their wildlife.

The second factor making this a great haven for wildlife, and one that is vital today, is the extent of the surrounding public land. GTNP itself is only about 300,000 acres, but it is completely surrounded by millions of acres of national forest, national park, and designated wilderness. Neighboring Yellowstone National Park is over two million acres, and the Bridger-Teton National Forest is almost three-and-a-half million acres. All together, about eighteen (18) or 20 million acres make up what is referred to as the Greater Yellowstone Ecosystem (GYE). This immense space of mountains, forests, and waterways gives wildlife room to migrate as they need, to spread out, and to establish territories. Some of the big predators such as grizzly bears, wolves, and mountain lions, for example, need these large areas of land in order to support enough individuals for a viable population. Over the past two centuries, the GYE has been a haven for a number of species that would have disappeared without protection of the land.

When this area was first proposed as a national park around 1898, it was largely to protect the thousands of elk that migrated out of Yellowstone and spent the winter in Jackson Hole. It would be another thirty years before GTNP was formed, but by then it was already a destination for visitors to see spectacular wildlife up close.

Bull moose

Common mergansers

Natural Communities

Visitors who look for wildlife in Grand Teton will quickly realize there are distinct types of habitat and vegetation in the park with certain animals that prefer those habitats. Elk can be observed leaving the forests in the evening and moving out into meadows to feed. Bison and pronghorns can be found on the sagebrush flats. Moose are usually found not far from willows and water. There are other physical conditions besides plants that can help pinpoint animals: pikas and marmots live in rocky slopes of mountain canyons; trumpeter swans often live on large beaver ponds; and American dippers nest on boulders and cliffs next to swift mountain streams. Experienced wildlife watchers know what each wild species needs for food, water, and protective vegetation and where those elements are to be found in the landscape.

Ecologists, those who study the relationship of living organisms with each other and with their environment, classify these habitats into groups they call biotic, or natural, communities. Ecologists name almost a dozen communities in the valley, but for the location and identification of Grand Teton's more common wildlife, we can divide the park into six general communities: aquatic, willow, meadow, sagebrush, forest, and alpine. There are no distinct lines between most communities, and the communities are all in the process of changing and evolving, so there are not many hard and fast rules about

Winter arrives in moose habitat.

Moose and American pelicans

where an animal might be seen. Some species, such as the raven, naturally travel between communities while other species, such as the river otter or the pine marten, can almost always be found in their preferred habitat.

These six communities are based on their dominant vegetation type, but obviously other types of plants grow in each of them. The reason vegetation type is used for naming a community group instead of an animal or geologic trait is that the plants tend to reflect the environmental conditions of soil, sun, water, and elevation—and ultimately the animals are dependent on those plants for survival. The other factor at work is plant succession—where communities change over time from one dominant species to another. Eventually, a climax species for those conditions takes over. Thus, a beaver pond may fill in with sediment to become a marsh, then as it dries to become a meadow it slowly fills in with willows, and finally spruce and fir trees take root and the area becomes a forest.

The reason all this is important in a search for wildlife in GTNP is that the plants indicate where the animals might be found. Their lives are intertwined so being able to identify and locate these natural communities will take you to wildlife throughout the year. For example, you might look for moose in the willows and spruce-fir forests in winter; near beaver ponds in spring and early summer; in the riverbottom forests or lower mountain canyons in mid-summer; back in the willows in fall; and out in the sagebrush flats in early winter.

Aquatic Communities

Beaver

An aquatic community is based on plants that grow in the water or on its surface and those that grow in the flooded, marshy land next to water. This includes ponds, streams, lakes, and quiet channels of rivers. An example is a beaver pond along the Moose-Wilson Road, covered with pond lilies. Tiny aquatic plants grow under water, reeds grow in shallow water along the shore, and sedges and rushes inhabit the muddy banks. Another good example is the Oxbow Bend near Moran, where an old channel of the Snake River is gradually silting in. The quiet water is filled with all kinds of floating and submerged plants, the shores and shallow flats grow reeds and rushes, and willows line the banks. Wildlife characteristic of the aquatic community includes fish, beavers, muskrats, ducks, geese, shorebirds, moose at certain times of the year, bald eagles, ospreys, kingfishers, and numerous smaller invertebrates and amphibians.

Willow Communities

Moose

This rich and diverse community is found along the banks of streams, at the edges of meadows, and in low areas where the water table is close to the surface. A wide variety of willow species may live in one place along with other shrubs, grasses, flowers, and a few water-tolerant trees. Willow thickets can grow so densely that they are impossible to walk through, but this makes them ideal for wildlife. Willow thickets are used by birds such as warblers, sparrows, and hummingbirds, and they are gnawed down and eaten by beavers. All kinds of rodents, from voles to gophers, can be found in the thick grasses and forbs that grow among the willows. Moose are the most noticeable inhabitants of this community, especially in winter when they rely almost exclusively on willows. Willow Flats Overlook, next to the Jackson Lake Lodge, and Blacktail Ponds Overlook near Moose are two good examples of the willow community.

Meadow Communities

Grand Teton National Park has a number of meadow types, ranging from small, dry alpine meadows to larger areas on the valley floor. Wherever they are found, water covers meadows part of the year, but, unlike marshes or bogs, meadows sit on solid ground below. They are characterized by grasses and sedges with a variety of smaller forbs (non-grasslike plants or herbs), and wildflowers. Most of the meadows in GTNP are relatively small and border other natural communities such as aquatic or forest, so at times they attract wildlife from those communities. The meadow community is utilized by all sorts of wildlife: elk and deer feed at night; bears dig up plant bulbs in spring and birds nest on the ground. Hawks and owls hunt for rodents, insects pollinate flowers, and the soil is rich with microscopic life. Good examples of meadows can be found between Oxbow Bend and the Moran Junction and along the road to the Death Canyon Trailhead.

Sagebrush Communities

Bison grazing in sagebrush five years after a wildfire

By far the largest and most obvious community in the park, sagebrush covers the expansive, well-drained gravel flats making up most of the valley floor. These flats are glacial outwash, laid down when receding glaciers deposited their round, rocky material. They have little topsoil. Sagebrush also grows on dry, lower hillsides. There are two species of sage and one species of bitterbrush that dominate the various communities, but at a glance they all look similiar. Near the edges of forests and toward the Snake River, the sagebrush community is slowly being invaded by individual trees, but few of them survive. One interesting thing about sagebrush is that wildfire kills it completely. Once an area is burned, it reverts to grasses and forbs and a few small shrubs, creating a rich grazing area for bison, elk, and pronghorns. Eventually the sage will return, but it will come from new plants outside the burn.

Wildlife in the sagebrush is abundant and includes such prominent mammals as the bison and pronghorn. Less noticeable are the badgers, coyotes, and numerous birds. In all, the sagebrush community is actually one of the biologically richest of the park. It holds a few species that are found nowhere else, such as the sage grouse. Elk migrate across it in fall and spring, birds of prey hunt there, and countless rodents burrow into its loose soil. Antelope Flats, looking east from the Glacier View Turnout on Highway 89/191 north of Moose, is prime sagebrush. *A meadow at the foot of the Tetons*

Forest Communities

Great gray owl

This large natural community is readily separated into smaller communities of different tree species, but they all serve the same purpose of offering cover and food for wildlife. The tree species also overlap in many places, so there are not always clear lines of community division. The overall forest community is composed of pines, firs, spruces, cottonwoods, and aspen—sometimes in relatively pure stands but more often in varying degrees of mixed forests. When we refer to a lodgepole pine forest, it means that they are the predominant species.

For the purpose of finding wildlife, we only need look at a few of the major tree communities. Lodgepole pine forms the largest forest communities. This tall, thin pine grows in dense stands on well-drained soil on the valley floor, foothills, and up the lower mountain slopes. It surrounds most of the large lakes in GTNP. Lodgepole pines live to be 100-200 years old. Elk bed down here in daytime, great gray owls nest in snags, and black bears feed on huckleberries in the open forest.

Douglas firs are massive when they mature and may live for 600 years. They inhabit smaller sites such as mountain ridges, dry meadows, and wind-swept slopes, and they often mix with other evergreens. Old Douglas firs are havens for cavity nesting birds, for perching golden eagles, and for tree dwellers such as the pine marten.

Spruce-fir forests, which contain both of those species and a few others, can be found in the rich, moist soil on moraines throughout the valley along the Snake River and in the lower canyons of the Tetons, continuing up into the rocky high country where the soil becomes sparse. Squirrels abound, as well as numerous small birds such as nuthatches, creepers, and woodpeckers. Porcupines live there as well as in lodgepole pine forests.

Cottonwood trees line the streams at lower elevations, especially along the Snake River, and aspen trees cover the low hills at the foot of the mountains. These open forests are especially important habitat for birds, deer, moose, elk, and members of the weasel family.

High in the mountains, where the trees end around 10,000 feet elevation, there are stands of hardy whitebark pines. These beautiful trees can readily be seen up at the head of Cascade Canyon. Their rich nut crop is vital to red squirrels and Clark's nutcrackers, who store the nuts in caches. Grizzly bears have made this food source one of their most important items, and in years when the crop is poor, the bears don't fare well. In early spring and again in fall, they locate and raid the squirrels' and nutcrackers' caches of this important food, sometimes locating and digging them up from under six feet of snow in the spring.

Alpine Communities

Bighorn sheep ram

From treeline, where trees no longer grow, up to the summits of the Teton peaks lies the alpine community. This mountainous landscape is cool and relatively moist in summer, with very little soil, and the winters are long and severe. The alpine plants are dwarfed and sturdy. Some grow in dense mats and many cling to bare rock or grow in crevices where soil has collected. In contrast to the sturdy and functional alpine plants, their blossoms are often delicate and brilliantly colored. Grasses, sedges, and small shrubs grow where there is enough soil, primarily in the upper canyons and basins.

Alpine wildlife is limited to those species that can cope with the harsh conditions, but it is well worth the hike into high country to observe them. Yellow-bellied marmots, pikas, and golden-mantled ground squirrels are all alpine species. Bighorn sheep, wolverines, and bears can be found at the lower levels of the alpine community. Alpine birds are largely migratory and leave the mountains for the winter. They include the golden eagle, black-rosy finch, and Clark's nutcracker.

Variations in Appearance

Wildlife doesn't always look like the photographs in field guides, so visitors often mistake one species for another, mistake males for females, or just can't put a name to an animal at all. Some visitors are surprised to learn that an animal's appearance can change dramatically from season to season.

One of the more striking examples is the group of mammals whose coats become white in winter and brown in summer. In GTNP, the short-tailed weasel (ermine) and long-tailed weasels gradually shed their white coats and grow a brown coat in spring. The snowshoe hare, a small hare of the mountain forests, also turns white in winter.

Some of the large animals, such as the elk, deer, and moose, shed their old fur in late winter and grow new coats. Moose are well-known for having a mangy appearance in the spring with big patches of old hair alternating with patches of lustrous, healthy hair. Elk and deer have a rich, reddish brown color early in the year, changing to grays and tans by winter. The males of these three animals also shed their antlers in late winter, and for a few months it may be difficult for inexperienced observers to tell males from females.

Birds go through changes of plumage from one to several times a year. This molting process grows new feathers to replace worn or broken ones, and it can also give the males brightly colored feathers for the mating season or give juvenile birds their first adult plumage. Bald eagles don't grow their characteristic adult plumage until they are four or five years and can be mistaken for golden eagles until then. Most field guides for birds point out these variations and changes.

A few species have a percentage of differently colored individuals referred to as a dark or "melanistic" phase. The yellow-bellied marmot of the Teton alpine community, for example, has a jet black phase. The Swainson's hawk, often seen near the sagebrush flats, also has a sooty black phase.

Individuals can vary considerably, as seen in the black bear. These animals vary from deep black to tan to a rich cinnamon color. They can also have white patches on their chests. Visitors unfamiliar with these variations often mistake brown-colored black bears for grizzlies.

Immature bald eagle

Adult bald ewagle

Mammals

Elk

Warm-blooded, covered with fur or hair, and nursing their young, mammals are the world's most highly evolved animals. In GTNP, they range from the tiny dwarf shrew, weighing less than an ounce, to the bison, which can grow to weigh almost a ton.

Mammals are divided into family groups depending on their similar physical features. These families include such collections as Deer (deer, elk, and moose), Dogs (coyote, wolf, fox), Cats (mountain lion, lynx, bobcat), Weasels (ermine, wolverine, skunk), and Squirrels (chipmunk, marmot, red squirrel). Each family has a scientific name to separate it from other, often similar families. Families are themselves grouped together under broader categories called Orders. Thus, all the families of squirrels, mice, beavers, porcupines, and gophers are in the order *Rodentia*, or rodents.

Mammals are an extremely diverse and interesting group of animals. They are also adaptable and intelligent. All mammals native to GTNP have found ways to survive or escape the harsh winter climate that limits or excludes other species. Marmots hibernate for eight months, pronghorns migrate out of the valley, and elk move down out of the high country.

Behavior of mammals is itself a fascinating subject. The animals display fear, threats, playfulness, submissiveness, and other expressions. By watching individuals over a period of a few hours, you can often witness how they communicate with each other and to other species. Some wildlife species live in large groups and have a social structure, while others live mostly solitary lives.

In looking for wildlife, go to the natural community they prefer. These are noted in the individual descriptions in the next section. These may change seasonally as the animals move about in search of food or to escape deep snowfall.

Even though they may seem tame and are accustomed to people, the mammals in Grand Teton National Park are wild. Their natural instincts for protecting themselves and their young will surface at unpredictable times if the animals are approached. Please enjoy them from a safe distance—especially moose, bison, and all bears.

A black bear cub is adapted to life in the forest.

Elk
Family Cervidae, Cervus elaphu

Description: Elk are very large members of the deer family. They have light tan hair, dark manes and legs, and light rump patches. In early summer their new coats have a reddish hue. Only the males have antlers, that they shed at the end of each winter and regrow in the spring and summer. While the new antlers are growing, they are covered with "velvet." Males are called bulls, females are cows, and young are calves.

Habits: Elk are herd animals and migrate between winter and summer ranges. In summer,they spend days in dense coniferous forests and graze in open meadows at night. The adult sex ratio is roughly three females to one male. In the fall breeding season, or "rut," the bulls bugle a challenge to other males and gather females into a harem. During winter, the cows and bulls generally stay apart in open meadows.

Where to Look: Elk can be observed emerging from forests into meadows at dusk, especially near Timbered Island, at the Elk Ranch meadows just south of Moran Junction, and along the Teton Park Road.

Details: Elk live to be about twelve to fifteen years old, but some may reach twenty or more.

Mule Deer
Family Cervidae, Odocoileus hemionu

Description: Mule deer have a white belly, throat and chin, a short tail tipped with black, and very large ears. In early summer their new coats are reddish brown, fading to gray by late autumn. Bucks have antlers that are shed in the winter and regrow in the spring and summer.

Habits: Mule deer migrate locally with the seasons. They are found in small groups that are larger in winter. They prefer to spend the day in forests and come out at dusk to feed in meadows.

Where to Look: Mule deer prefer mixed forests of aspen and pine, hillside meadows, and south facing slopes in winter. Look for them on the park's moraines and along trails into the canyons, and near Lupine Meadows, Leigh Lake Trail, and Signal Mountain area.

Details: Males are called bucks, females are does, and young are fawns. They live from five to ten years of age in the wild.

Moose
Family Cervidae, *Alces alces*

Description: Moose are the largest members of the Deer family, as big as a horse, with a heavy body and long legs. A moose has large ears, a long head and muzzle, a dewlap hanging from the throat, and an almost black coat that fades over winter. Only the bulls have antlers that they lose in winter and regrow in spring and summer.

Habits: Moose are mostly solitary except for small family groups and in winter when a dozen or more may gather where there is food. Individuals use the same ranges seasonally and are most active at dusk and dawn. In summer they aren't far from water. They are possessive of their space, and will attack intruders—human or otherwise. Moose were very rare in northwestern Wyoming in the mid-1800s, and were absent from Jackson Hole until the early 1900s.

Where to Look: Moose can be found from the high spruce-fir forests down to willow and riparian areas. In winter they prefer willow thickets and sage flats. Look for them in beaver ponds, along the Snake River, and at the Blacktail Ponds Overlook. The Oxbow Bend area is prime moose habitat.

Details: Males are called bulls, females are cows, and young are calves. The oldest known moose was age twenty-seven.

Pronghorn
Family Antilocapridae, *Antilocapra americana*

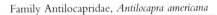

Description: Pronghorn are delicate, deer-like animals with a solid body and long legs. They have large heads and eyes. Their bodies are white underneath, rusty brown to tan above with black and dark markings on heads and necks. Their rumps are white, and they have blackish horns with anterior prongs. Females have short horns without prongs.

Habits: Pronghorn are active day and night, mostly just after sunrise and before sunset. They live in open grassland and sage. Large males are territorial and gather females into bands. They are social animals, and in central Wyoming can form herds of 1,000 animals. Wyoming has the largest populations of pronghorn in North America.

Where to Look: In the park, they prefer grasslands and sagebrush on Antelope Flats. Look for them in old hayfields from Kelly to Moose, near Lupine Meadows and in other wide open spaces.

Details: Pronghorn are commonly called antelope. Males are bucks, females are does, and young are fawns. Under ideal conditions they may live ten years.

Bison

Family Bovidae, *Bos bison*

Description: There's no mistaking bison—one of the largest mammals in North America—with their massive heads, high shoulder humps, short necks and snout, short round black horns, and blackish-brown coats. Calves of the year have a burnt orange coat for the first month or so. Both sexes have horns.

Habits: Bison seem always to be either eating, walking, or both at the same time. They are also known for their wallowing behavior—rolling on the ground and making clouds of dust. They are herd animals, but older bulls can be found alone. Bison may seem docile but are very unpredictable, and bulls often charge without warning.

Where to Look: Bison occupy grasslands and meadows and move into adjoining forests at times. In the park, they are most common on Antelope Flats between Kelly and Moose and Elk Ranch Flats. They are especially drawn to areas of wildfire as new vegetation begins to grow.

Details: Bison are commonly called buffalo. Males are bulls, females are cows, and young are calves. They may live to be 15-20 in the wild.

Black Bear

Family Ursidae, *Ursus americanus*

Description: Black bears have a variety of colors—cinnamon, black, brown, and blond. They have relatively short claws, and their footprints seldom leave claw marks.

Habits: Black bears are most active at dusk and dawn, but their late day activity can continue well into the night. They are usually solitary except for females with cubs. In their winter dens, they do not hibernate as deeply as small mammals; instead, they hibernate and awaken at times. Black bears feed on vegetation—grass, berries, and roots—and insects and carrion. In spring, they actively prey on young elk and deer.

Where to Look: Black bears prefer the mountains, canyons, and forests. They like forests with a thick understory of shrubs and grasses. They are excellent tree climbers. In the park, they are most often seen in the forests of the canyon and at the foot of the mountains. Look in Death Canyon, Cascade Canyon, and on the open, lower mountain slopes above Lupine Meadows at dawn.

Details: Bears have extremely good memories, especially for food sources, which is why they should never get human food. Age twenty-five is old for a black bear.

Grizzly Bear

Family Ursidae, *Ursus arctos*

Description: Grizzlies can be distinguished from black bears by their prominent shoulder humps, their hair that may have gray or white tips, and face profiles that are more "dished." They are most often a tan or light brown color. Grizzlies have longer claws than black bears, and their tracks show it.

Habits: Grizzlies feed on a variety of foods, largely vegetation in summer, and they actively prey on mice, ground squirrels, and elk fawns in spring. At various times, they concentrate on eating moths, pine nuts, gophers, or plant tubers. Like black bears, they are most active at dawn and from dusk into the night. Grizzlies hibernate in dens from November until late March to early May. They do not hibernate as soundly as smaller mammals and may awaken at times. Grizzlies are a rare and "threatened" species.

Where to Look: Grizzlies can be found in varied habitat—they prefer meadows, grasslands, open forests, and stream bottoms. Grizzlies are seen throughout the park in meadows, along streams or lakes, at the forest edge, and on high, open slopes.

Details: A grizzly's hair often has light-colored tips, giving it a "grizzled" look. Oldtimers called the bears "silvertips." Grizzlies have lived to age twenty-five in the wild, and can live to forty or more in captivity.

How to Tell a Grizzly from a Black Bear

While biologists use many subtle physical features and behaviors to identify bears, there are a couple of basic clues to help. Color doesn't always work since both species occur in a range of colors.

1. Black bears have a straight profile from ears to nose while a grizzly is somewhat concave.

2. Grizzlies have a "hump" above the front shoulders that gives their body a more evenly weighted look. Black bears often appear to have a larger hind end because they lack this shoulder hump.

3. While both species inhabit many of the same areas, grizzlies tend to forage in meadows and open areas, while black bears tend to prefer the forests.

Coyote

Family Canidae, *Canis latrans*

Description: Coyotes are medium to large-sized dog-like animals, with a banded appearance of blended gray and a little black mixed with reddish tints, and buff underparts. Their long pointy ears are usually erect, and they have furry tails with a black tip.

Habits: Like many successful animals, coyotes can survive on just about anything. They are carnivores who hunt mice and ground squirrels and scavenge large animals that have died. They eat insects and plants when they need to. They are usually most active at dusk and dawn. Coyotes form packs near abundant food, but are less social than wolves.

Where to Look: Coyotes adapt to most habitats, and they travel frequently in search of food. They can be seen just about anywhere in the park. Look for them in meadows and open areas in the sagebrush, along streams, and on the rolling hills in the eastern part of the park.

Details: The coyotes' natural intelligence and persistence make them popular characters in Native American storytelling. Most coyotes only live three to ten years. While once common, coyotes are now seldom seen.

Gray Wolf

Family Canidae, *Canis lupus*

Description: This is the largest member of the Dog family, with long legs,

large feet, and a long, straight tail. The wolf's face has wide tufts of fur projecting down and outward below ears. Their fur color varies from grayish-white to black.

Habits: Wolves live in packs, with their dens used only for the birth and care of their young. They are very social. In winter they move often and may go long distances. Wolves are rare in the park and are seldom seen unless they are near their dens. They are most active at dusk or dawn.

Where to Look: Wolves prefer the open topography of the eastern side of the park to the sheer slopes and peaks of the Tetons, but they roam constantly and can be found in any habitat. Antelope Flats and the area from Elk Ranch meadows to Two Ocean Lake road are both good wolf habitats.

Details: Wolves are noticeably taller and rangier than coyotes, with large heads. Coyotes run with their tails down, while wolves run with tails horizontally. Wolves may live to be fifteen or sixteen.

American Badger
Family Mustelidae, *Taxidea taxus*

Description: The badger is a stout, short-legged, flat-bodied animal of the grassland and sagebrush. They are about 2½ to three feet long, and are a grayish color tinged with brown. Their snouts, tops of their heads, and cheeks are black, with distinct white stripes down the faces. They have extremely long front claws.

Habits: Badgers are usually nocturnal and stay underground during daylight, but in the springtime they are often out near their dens with their young. Badgers do not hibernate and may pile dirt up on top of the snow when they dig below after their prey of ground squirrels, voles, or any other burrowing animal.

Where to Look: Badgers are burrowers and prefer relatively deep soil, so they are most common in the grass and sagebrush areas in the eastern part of the park. Look very early and late in the day along the entire Antelope Flats Road, Mormon Row, and in the Elk Ranch meadows south of Moran Junction.

Details: Badgers and coyotes sometimes hunt cooperatively—the coyote chasing down prey that the badger has unearthed, or the badger digging up prey that the coyote has chased into a burrow.

Pacific Marten
Family Mustelidae, *Martes caurina*

Description: The marten is a house-cat sized weasel, long and slender, with a bushy tail, pointy face, golden brown fur with darker legs and tail, and a yellow or orange patch on throat and upper chest.

Habits: The marten is solitary except during breeding season. They communicate with vocalizations and scents and are active year round although they may den during extremely low temperatures. They are often seen up in the trees, but most of their time is actually spent on the forest floor.

Where to Look: The forests along the base of the Tetons are prime marten habitat. The Valley Trail, especially where it passes through spruce-fir forests, is a likely place to see them. Martens occasionally den in old log structures, sheds, and barns in the park.

Details: Martens have been documented eating over one hundred different kinds of foods.

Short-Tailed Weasel

Family Mustelidae, *Mustela ermine*

Description: Commonly known as the ermine, the short-tailed weasel is one of two similar animals in the park. The other is the long-tailed weasel. Both are small, elongated animals, but the short-tailed is about seven to thirteen inches long and the long-tailed is eleven to twenty-one inches in length. Both species grow new fur to turn white in winter and brown in summer.

Habits: Weasels can be active at any time, but tend to prefer the daylight hours. They are carnivores, and are ferocious hunters. The short-tailed weasel eats mostly mice and chipmunks, while the larger long-tailed catches prey as large as hares and grouse.

Where to Look: Weasels are found in most habitat types and are most abundant where there is lots of their prey—mixed forests, meadows, sagebrush, and foothills. In the park they are often seen darting under older log buildings and historic structures.

Details: The ermine's color changes are determined by the season but not by the weather—if snowfall arrives late the white ermine may not blend in at all.

American Beaver

Family Castoridae, *Castor canadensis*

Description: The familiar beaver is Wyoming's largest rodent. It is dark brown or red-brown with a large, flat scaly tail. Its hind toes are webbed, and it has prominent front teeth.

Habits: Beavers cut down trees with their incisor teeth and use the limbs to build a dam across running water. They build mound-like lodges with underwater entrances, or they burrow into a stream bank to make a lodge. Beavers are generally nocturnal and active all year, living in small colonies of four to eight related individuals.

Where to Look: Beavers are common all along the Snake River and its riparian surroundings. Look especially where there are willows, aspens, and cottonwoods: Sawmill Ponds, Oxbow Bend, Swabacher Landing and numerous ponds in the north end of the park.

Details: When a beaver is disturbed, it slaps its tail on the water to warn other beavers as it dives underwater.

Common Muskrat

Family Cricetidae, *Ondatra zibethicus*

Description: The muskrat is a large rodent with a long, skinny tail that is flattened laterally like a rudder, and dark brown or blackish fur.

Habits: Muskrats lead a semi-aquatic life like the beaver but do not build dams. Their houses are either cone-shaped piles of mud and vegetation or burrows in a bank. They are most active at night and during dark, rainy days. They eat aquatic vegetation and roots, especially cattails.

Where to Look: Muskrats occupy most aquatic habitats including creeks, seeps, lakes, marshes, and ponds. Look in beaver ponds, at Oxbow Bend, and at Christian Pond.

Details: Muskrats can close their lips behind their front teeth so they can gnaw underwater.

A beaver chewed tree.

How to Tell a Beaver from a Muskrat

When it is swimming, a muskrat uses its tail like a rudder. You'll see the long, narrow tail snaking along behind. The beaver's tail is as broad as the body and usually doesn't show when the animal is swimming.

If the animals are out of the water, the muskrat is much smaller and quick-moving. Beavers are quite large and move more slowly unless frightened. The beaver's tail is very obvious.

While muskrats may live in marshes or in meadow streams, the beaver will usually not be found unless there is a supply of willows, trees, or large shrubs nearby.

Beavers build dams and large stick and mud lodges, while the muskrat builds only a small, cone shaped lodge of mud and aquatic vegetation. Beavers leave telltale signs of peeled sticks, gnawed tree limbs, and felled trees.

North American River Otter Family Mustelidae, *Lutra canadensis*

Description: Otters are semi-aquatic animals with short legs and solid, tapering tails. They have a smallish, flattened head with a blunt face. Their color ranges from pale chestnut to dark brown on their backs and silver gray on their bellies. In the water, they look almost black. Otters are in the same family with weasels, badgers, and skunks. They are carnivores, and nearly all of their diet is freshly caught fish.

Habits: Otters are active any time of day, peaking at dusk and dawn. They use dens dug out by other animals or natural shelters along the waterways.

Where to Look: Otters are most abundant in the Snake River and are often seen at the Oxbow Bend area or just below the Jackson Lake Dam.

Details: Otters are intelligent, playful animals and can be seen sliding on snow in the winter or tumbling and wrestling in the shallow water.

North American Porcupine Family Erethizontidae, *Erethizon dorsatum*

Description: These large rodents with their stout, rounded bodies, short feet, thick muscular tails, and quills are easy to identify when you see one.

Habits: Porcupines are solitary and slow-moving. They are active all year, usually at night, and feed on tree bark, shoots and buds, and other vegetation. They den in caves, hollow logs, and under old buildings.

Where to Look: Anywhere in the forests along the foot of the Tetons is good porcupine habitat. Watch for telltale whitish, freshly gnawed bark near the tops of pine and spruce trees.

Details: Porcupines do not throw their quills, but when the animals are frightened, their quills detach more easily. An average adult porcupine has about 30,000 quills on its body. American Indians use dyed quills to make intricate, beautiful decorations on clothing and for certain jewelry.

ellow-bellied Marmot

Family Sciuridae, *Marmota flaviventris*

Description: Marmots are large, heavy-bodied rodents. Their fur is brown to yellowish, an orange to yellowish belly, and they have relatively long tails.

Habits: Marmots are colonial and live in complex tunnel systems under the rocks. They hibernate eight months of the year, from September to May. uring the summer months, they feed constantly on vegetation. They love sun themselves on rocks.

Where to Look: Marmots occur at all altitudes in the park, from the alpine gion to the foothills. They are most commonly seen along trails leading to the mountains and are often seen along the trail to Taggart Lake.

Details: There is also a beautiful, jet-black variety in the Tetons. This is a melanistic" color phase of the same species.

merican Pika

Family Ochotonidae, *Ochotona princeps*

ika haystack

Description: Pikas are a bit larger than a guinea pig with short legs and no tails and prominent, almost circular ears. Their color varies from chalky gray to brown. They look somewhat rabbit-like.

Habits: Pikas are active year-round, usually in the morning, as they cut and pile food and store it in small "haystacks" under large boulders. They do not hibernate but eat their stored "hay" of grasses and wildflowers. Their call is a unique whistle, described as a high-pitched bleat that is difficult to pinpoint.

Where to Look: Never far from talus slopes or outcrops of rock, pikas are most often seen in the mountain canyons. Look in rocky areas along he trail into Cascade Canyon, Death Canyon, or Paintbrush Canyon. The Iidden Falls area is also good.

Details: Pikas have a second, smaller set of incisor teeth right behind their ront ones.

Least Chipmunk

Family Sciuridae, *Neotamius minim*

Description: This is one of three chipmunk species in the park. All have stripes on their backs, but the least and the Yellow-pine chipmunk have black as the outermost line. Tl Uinta chipmunk has a white stripe a the outer stripe. This least chipmunk is the smallest and runs with its tail up in the air. Often confused for golden-mantled ground squirrel.

Habits: Chipmunks are common in dry, open forests with fallen logs and underbrush and in rocky areas in the sagebrush.

Where to Look: Chipmunks are common along many of the park's hiking trails in the valley and along the base of the mountains. They are abundant around developed areas such as campgrounds and trailheads.

Details: Chipmunks store piles of food for the winter and awaken from their deep sleep to eat.

Uinta Ground Squirrel

Family Sciuridae, *Spermophilus armatu*

Description: This squirrel-sized roder is brown with fine flecks of gray and black. It has a rusty-cinnamon nose and shoulders and a straight, mediun sized tail.

Habits: These ground squirrels are common in the sagebrush and grassy areas of the park, especially in camp-grounds, trailheads, and developed areas. They are often seen standing erect beside their burrows or scurrying through the sagebrush. Their call is a shrill, chirping whistle.

Where to Look: Look in the sagebrush near park facilities and at scenic turnouts. They are common around the Menors Ferry area, near Christian Pond, and along Mormon Row.

Details: Uinta ground squirrels have many common names, including "chiseler" and "picket-pin." In summer, they are the chief prey of several predators including hawks, coyotes, and badgers. Although primarily vegetarians, these ground squirrels occasionally "cannibalize" other Uintas that have been killed on park roads.

Red Squirrel

Family Sciuridae, *Tamiasciurus hudsonicus*

Description: This small, distinctively brownish-red squirrel has white underparts and a pronounced lateral black stripe separating the white belly from its upper colors. It also has white eye rings.

Habits: This little squirrel defends its territory against other red squirrels and is quite vocal with its aggressive "chatter." It is often seen running along fallen trees or sitting up in a tree limb.

Where to Look: All the pine and spruce-fir forests of the park have these squirrels. Look along the Hidden Falls, Leigh Lake, or along the Valley Trail.

Details: These squirrels are responsible for the occasional pine cone that drops out of the trees onto the hiking trail.

Golden-mantled Ground Squirrel

Family Sciuridae, *Spermophilus lateralis*

Description: In size, golden-mantled ground squirrels are between a chipmunk and a squirrel. They look like large chipmunks but have no stripes on their heads. On each side, they have a single white stripe bordered on both edges by a black stripe. Their heads and shoulders are reddish-brown.

Habits: These ground squirrels live in small colonies or as individuals and hibernate all winter. They feed on vegetation, insects, and bird eggs. Mushrooms and other fungi and leaves of flowering plants make up most of their diet. Their hibernation is almost three months shorter than the Uinta ground squirrel's.

Where to Look: In the mountains and canyons, they prefer rocky areas in the pine forests or high meadows and alpine habitats. They are fairly common along the park trails, especially in Cascade Canyon around Inspiration Point.

Details: Their heads and shoulders are the same rich golden color so the animals appear to be wearing a "mantle." The young, born about the first of June in litters of two to eight, are almost full-grown in two months.

Red

Seldom Seen Creatures

Some of the park's wildlife are rarely observed. This may be due to their elusive nature, low populations, or nocturnal habits. For example, most owl and bat species are seldom seen, pocket gophers are plentiful but rarely come above ground, and flying squirrels are nocturnal. Wolverines exist in very limited numbers in the Tetons, but occasionally a backcountry hiker will see one. Some of these rarer species are a thrill to see, and their continued presence in the park is important to verify—they should be reported to park rangers if observed.

Red Fox   Family Canidae, *Vulpes vulpes*

Description: The familiar red fox is a small, dog-like animal with pointed features. Its fur is a yellowish red with black "stockings" on the legs and a large, bushy, white-tipped tail.
Habits and Habitat: Red foxes prefer the brush and forest understory, streambanks, and generally less open terrain than coyotes. They often den close to human activity under old buildings or in empty marmot or badger burrows. Mormon Row and Antelope Flats, as well as the Snake River corridor, have red foxes. While once uncommon, these animals are now seen frequently aournd Moose and Colter Bay.

Canada Lynx

Family Felidae, *Felis lynx*

Description: A large cat, bobcat size but heavier looking, and much smaller than a mountain lion, the lynx has distinctly tufted ears, large cheek ruffs of pale hair, and a short, black-tipped tail. The lynx has huge feet for its size.
Habits and Habitat: The lynx prefers the deep, remote forests, where it lives year-round. Their favorite prey is the snowshoe hare, and lynx populations are tied to those of the hare. Lynx are largely nocturnal. In the park, lynx have been spotted near the Snake River and near the northern boundary. While there are no official sightings in the park, lynx have been documented in Yellowstone National Park, and could show up here.

Bighorn Sheep

Family Bovidae, *Ovis canadensis*

Description: A stocky, muscular sheep about six feet long, a bighorn is brown with a white belly, rump, muzzle, and eye patch. Rams have massive, curled horns when they are older, and females have slender, uncurled horns.
Habits and Habitat: Bighorns live in alpine meadows and high slopes, moving down to lower elevations in winter to find open grass. Some bands of sheep winter on high, south-facing mountain sides. In the park, they are found in the southern end of the Tetons.

Snowshoe Hare

Family Leporidae, *Lepus americanus*

Description: These interesting animals are not seen too often, but there's no mistaking them. Related to rabbits, snowshoe hares have large hind feet, dark brown fur flecked with buff, and small ears. In winter, they turn all white except for their black ear tips.
Habits and Habitat: Snowshoe hares forage on the ground during the night and rest in dense thickets or under trees during the day.
Where to Look: These hares prefer shrubby habitats including aspen, willow, and conifers in the mountains. Along the canyon trails, look for them sitting quietly under trees and shrubs.
Details: Snowshoe hares are the main prey of lynxes, and the cats' populations rise and fall with the numbers of hares.

Meadow Vole
Family Cricetidae, *Microtus pennsylvanic*

Description: Voles are small, dark rodents some what like mice. They have very small eyes, a tiny tail, and a roundish body that seems to look the same coming or going.
Habits and Habitat: These small rodents live in the grass, where they tunnel little pathways under the vegetation and pile it into nests under flat rocks, old boards, or anything else left lying flat on the ground.
Where to Look: Voles are found in grassy areas in the sagebrush, in meadows, and in grassy clearings in the aspen and cottonwood forests. Mormon Row, and Antelope Flats have many voles.
Details: Voles are one of the major prey species of hawks, coyotes, badgers and other predators.

Mountain Lion
Family Felidae, *Felis concol*

Description: There's no mistaking the mountai lion. They are up to eight or nine feet long including the tail. Their color is a uniform gra to rufous brown with a whitish belly, throat, and chin. The tail is thick and long.
Habits and Habitat: Mountain lions are most active just after dusk and just before dawn, bu occasionally they extend their activity well int daylight hours. They prefer to prey on deer ar other large game and follow those herds throughout the year. In winter, mountain lions will follow deer and elk down to low elevations near civilization. Seeing a mountain lion in the wild requires a good deal of luck, bu hillsides and ridges from Colter Bay to the eastern border near Moran are a possibility.

American Mink
Family Mustelidae, *Mustela viso*

Description: The mink is a medium-sized weasel (about two feet long and weighing two to three pounds) that lives and hunts in and around the water. They are a uniform deep, rich brown and look black when wet.
Habits and Habitat: Mink are nocturnal for the most part, but can be observed early and late in the day. They are most often seen along the banks of the Snake River, where they hunt for mice, frogs, birds, and snakes. Oxbow Bend is also a likely area.

Northern Pocket Gopher   Family Geomyidae, *Thamomys talpoides*

Description: Pocket gophers are medium-sized rodents with small eyes, ears, and snout. They have large front claws for digging, and fur-lined cheek pouches, or pockets, for carrying food through their tunnels.
Habits and Habitat: Specialized for life underground, pocket gophers live solitary lives in a maze of tunnels. Most of their diet consists of plant roots, tubers, and runners. They rarely come to the surface, but they leave signs that indicate how common and widespread they are in the park. Look in meadows or sagebrush flats for long, snake-like eskers of dirt on the ground. These tubes are left from gopher tunnels made in winter beneath the snow.

Wolverine   Family Mustelidae, *Gulo gulo*

Description: A large, stocky member of the Weasel family, the wolverine is roughly three feet long and weighs thirty to forty pounds. Their fur is blackish brown with an indistinct reddish brown stripe on each side. They have long guard hairs that give them a shaggy appearance. Wolverines appear to be clumsy, walking with their backs arched and heads and tails down. These animals have been observed in the high alpine country, in canyons and forests.

Little Brown Bat   Family Vespertilionidae, *Myotis lucifugus*

Description: A small, dark mammal with leathery wings, the bat is a familiar image to most people. This particular bat is only about three to four inches long and has a bronze sheen to its back.
Habits and Habitat: Little brown bats are common in many of the park's older log buildings, especially historic cabins that are not in use. The Jenny Lake area and the Signal Mountain Lodge area are good places to look at dusk, especially near outdoor lights.

White-tailed Deer   Family Cervidae, *Odocoileus virginianus*

Description: This deer can be told apart from the more common mule deer by their long, bushy white tails and their long thin legs. The males have antlers formed by a curving main beam with tines that do not fork. When white-tails run, their large white tails are held upright like a flag.
Habits and Habitat: These deer are seen occasionally in meadows and brushy streamside habitat. They are rarely observed in the coniferous forests or in the higher mountains where mule deer go.

A great blue heron fishing in a beaver pond.

Birds

The sighting of a wild bird species evokes a passion in some visitors that, for them, approaches the thrill of climbing mountains. Some "birders" will spend their entire vacations peering into shrubs at dawn or sitting patiently for hours by a stand of dead trees, looking for that new bird to add to their lifetime list of sightings. But many "non-birder" visitors to GTNP are just as excited to see a bald eagle perched in a tall spruce tree, an osprey diving into the Snake River to emerge with a trout, or an American dipper plunging into the swift water of Cascade Creek. Birds in GTNP range in size from the tiny calliope hummingbird to the huge and graceful trumpeter swan.

Birds are not only colorful and fun to observe, but they exhibit behavior that tells much more about the natural history of the park. Sage grouse perform their mating dance each spring; cowbirds ride on the backs of bison; magpies and ravens gather at the carcasses of winter-killed elk; and three-toed woodpeckers arrive in flocks to areas of forest that burned the previous year.

There are year-round residents, and there are migratory species that only spend a few months here in summer to nest. The mountain chickadee moves from the mountain forest down to the valley, while the yellow-headed blackbird leaves for Mexico. There are also birds that pass through on their way somewhere else, and a few that are blown in on storms.

Birds have adapted to every habitat in every natural community in the park. They nest among the rocks in the highest alpine meadows, and they hollow out trees in the dense spruce-fir forests. Each of the natural communities listed previously in this book hosts its own variety of birds as well as some that are common in several communities.

The birds' diets, nesting habits, and behaviors have all evolved to fit a particular habitat. For some birds, a slight change in vegetation or prey species can have a disastrous effect. For that reason, park managers work at keeping the entire ecosystem of the area intact, with all of its natural processes and resources. As with the mammals, birds are divided into orders, families, and then genus and species.

A pair of trumpeter swans and their cygnet.

Western Grebe
Family Podicipedidae, *Aechmophorus occidentalis*

Description: Grebes are loon-like waterbirds, but with long, erect necks. Western Grebes are recognized by their dark bodies and long, white and black necks. They are graceful on water but awkward on land.

Habits: These are open-water diving birds, and because of their ability to stay under for a long time, they may seem to disappear when you try to identify them. They are usually found in small numbers, pairs, or individually.

Where to Look: Western Grebes are commonly seen on Jenny Lake, Jackson Lake, Oxbow Bend, and Two Ocean Lake. Look far out in the center of the lakes.

American White Pelican
Family Pelicanidae, *Pelecanus erythrorhynchos*

Description: At a distance this huge bird might look like a swan, but the immense bill makes it unmistakable. All white, with a yellow-orange bill and black trailing edges during the breeding season on its wings identify this bird.

Habits: Pelicans in the park are usually seen floating or swimming in small groups on open water, flying gracefully up and down the Snake River, or circling in numbers very high overhead. They swim and dive for fish but do not dive from the air.

Where to Look: The exposed mud flats of the Oxbow Bend are good locations as well as the Snake River just below the Jackson Lake Dam. The northern end of Jackson Lake is also a good place to find pelicans.

Great Blue Heron
Family Ardeidae, *Ardea herodius*

Description: The Great blue heron is a large gray blue bird of waterways, marshes, and ponds. It has a long pointed bill, a dark crown, and a few black plumes on the back of its head. Its long legs may be hidden in water or vegetation.

Habits: Herons may stand motionlessly at the water's edge, waiting for fish, amphibians, insects, or other prey. If disturbed, they will leap into the air with a squawk and fly off low over the water. Great blue herons nest in large, treetop colonies.

Where to Look: Herons are often seen by visitors taking a raft trip on the Snake River. These birds are also common in the Oxbow Bend area and along the Gros Ventre River at the park's southern border.

Trumpeter Swan
Family Anatidae, *Cygnus buccinator*

Description: This rare white swan is the largest waterfowl in North America. They are all white except for their black bills and feet. Juvenile birds are grayish brown and have pinkish bills with a black base. Trumpeter swans have wingspans of almost seven feet.
Habits: In spring and summer they are seen swimming on beaver ponds and floating along streams through marshlands. They dip to feed on aquatic vegetation. Trumpeter swans nest on islands in beaver ponds or marshes, sometimes on top of beaver lodges.
Where to Look: Always around water, trumpeter swans are year-round residents and only move to find open water in winter. They will gather in winter along the Snake River or on streams with warm spring water that do not freeze. Look in large ponds and small lakes in the park, especially Oxbow Bend, Christian Pond, National Elk Refuge, and Swan Lake.

Canada Goose
Family Anatidae, *Branta canadensis*

Description: This is the same large goose found commonly throughout the United States, with its brown body, black head and neck, and bright white cheeks. The bill and legs are black. They are usually seen in flocks and often on the ground.
Habits: Canada geese nest all over the valley—along the Snake River, in the National Elk Refuge, and around Jackson Lake. They nest on the ground as well as in old hawk nests in trees and cliffs, and on islands. The goslings begin to hatch in early May.
Where to Look: The north end of Jackson Lake is usually a good place to find geese, as well as the open fields of the old Elk Ranch, just south of Moran Junction. Oxbow Bend is good for all waterfowl species.

Barrow's Goldeneye

Family Anatidae, *Bucephala islandic*

Description: There are two goldeneye species here (named for their eye color), and they are often mixed together. Females can be hard to te apart, but the males are easier. The Barrow's is black and white with a large, roundish-looking head. It has a large white crescent spot between the eye and the bill. The common goldeneye has more white than black on the body with a large, *white round spot* between the eye and bill.

Habits: The Barrow's is here year-round, and inhabits open water. It is a diving duck, popping up and disappearing again as it feeds.

Where to Look: Lakes and ponds, such as the Oxbow Bend, Two Ocean Lake, and Jackson Lake are good sites. In winter, the Barrow's goldeneye can be found on the Snake River.

Common Merganser

Family Anatidae, *Mergus merganse*

Description: Mergansers are low-floating, long-bodied ducks. They have a grayish body and reddish head with a short crest that looks almo like unkempt hair. During the winter and early summer, the males are mostly all white with a dark green–black head. Both sexes have long, narrow, orange bills.

Habits: These diving ducks are common on lakes and rivers where they swim, dive, and often sit and sun on the shores.

Where to Look: Any of the lakes in the park are possible sites, but mergansers are almost always around the Oxbow Bend, northern Jackson Lake, an on the Snake River.

Mallard

Family Anatidae, *Anas platyrhyncho*

Description: These large, familiar ducks are found all across the United States but may look "exotic" to visitors not expecting to see them here. The male's glossy green head, white neck band, and dark brown chest stand out, and a closer look reveals a white tail with a few curled, black feathers on top. The females are a mottled brown.

Habits: These ducks are "dabblers" and prefer shallow water, creeks, and ponds where they can tip up and reach the bottom without diving. They are often seen swimming close to the shores of ponds or in small creeks.

Where to Look: Any of the park's waterways could hold mallards, from tiny spring creeks at the Blacktail Ponds Overlook to the muddy shores of the Oxbow Bend.

Red-tailed Hawk

Family Accipitridae, *Buteo jamaicensis*

Description: This is the most common large hawk in the park and is often seen on telephone poles, tree limbs, or fence posts. The adult has a dark brown body and head with a pale breast and a red tail. The tail is only red on the upper side, but the color usually shows through if the hawk soars overhead.

Habits: Red-tailed hawks hunt for mice and voles in the park's meadows and open fields. When not perched, they soar in lazy circles overhead.

Where to Look: The eastern half of the park, with its former ranchland and old homestead farms, is ideal. Look along Mormon Row and the entire Antelope Flats Road.

Northern Harrier

Family Accipitridae, *Circus cyaneus*

Description: This is a large hawk of the park's meadows and open grassland areas. It has a long, slender body, tail, and wings. The harrier has a distinctive white rump at the base of the tail. Males are gray and females are a mottled brown.

Habits: Harriers fly and glide low over the open ground, twisting suddenly to dive into the grass to catch their prey of mice, snakes, frogs, and small birds.

Where to Look: The open fields of the Antelope Flats area, along Mormon Row, and the old ranchlands near the Gros Ventre campground are all good sites.

Swainson's Hawk

Family Accipitridae, *Buteo swainsoni*

Description: The Swainson's hawk is similar to the red-tailed hawk but has a few key differences. When viewed in flight from below, the Swainson's hawk's wings show distinct, dark feathers on the trailing half. It has a light face with a dark head, and a dark red breast. Swainson's hawks also have a "melanistic" color phase that is a dark, sooty brown and rust.

Habits: These hawks have habits similar to red-tailed hawks, perching in trees and on fence posts or soaring overhead.

Where to Look: Swainson's hawks are often seen perched in trees not far from the highway, between the park's south entrance and Moose.

American Kestrel
Family Falconidae, *Falco sparveriu*

Description: Roughly robin-sized, this small falcon has beautiful facial markings—vertical black and creamy white lines mixed with blue and gray on top. Their backs are rusty brown with black bars, and the male has blue-gray wings. Like all falcons, they have slender, pointed wings that give them a swift flight.

Habits: Kestrels are commonly seen on telephone poles and perched at the top of dead trees.

Where to Look: These little falcons are found throughout the park in open areas and along the border between sagebrush flats and forest. Teton Park Road has many old snags along its length where kestrels often perch.

Greater Sage-Grouse
Family Phasianidae, *Centrocercus urophasianus*

Description: Sage grouse are large, fairly non-descript birds with a gray speckled appearance that matches the sagebrush. They have long, pointed tails, white undersides to their wings, and black bellies. During the spring mating season, the male has a black throat and yellow combs above its eyes.

Habits: These birds are secretive and difficult to see except when they take to the air. They are also visible during their spectacular spring mating ritual when the males puff out large white throat sacs, fan their tails, and strut for the hens.

Where to Look: These are strictly sagebrush birds. Antelope Flats Road is good as well as along Highway 89/187 near the Jackson Hole Airport.

Dusky Grouse
Family Phasianidae, *Dendragapus obscurus*

Description: A dark, camouflaged forest bird, the dusky grouse is the size of a chicken and often about as tame. The female is speckled brown and white, and the speckled gray male has a distinct orange patch above each eye. In mating season, the male fans its tail and inflates reddish purple air sacs on its throat.

Habits: These grouse are often seen crossing hiking trails in the park but difficult to see if they don't move.

Where to Look: Dusky grouse inhabit most of the park's conifer forests. The summit of Signal Mountain has historically been a good place to see these birds, either along the roadway or on the pathways at the top.

andhill Crane

Family Gruidae, *Grus canadensis*

Description: Standing almost four feet tall, the sandhill crane is a beautiful all-gray bird with a red cap on its head. Through the summer the crane's body and neck feathers become stained a rusty brown. The crane's deep, trumpeting call sounds almost prehistoric.

Habits: In early summer, the birds are seen in small flocks and pairs in meadows and marshy eas. They are here to mate and nest. They feed in open meadows d wetlands.

Where to Look: Cranes frequent the Willow Flats area near Jackson Lake am, the Snake River bottomlands, and Oxbow Bend.

illdeer

Family Charadriidae, *Charadrius vociferus*

Description: An orange-brown robin-sized bird with long legs, the killdeer has two distinct black bands across its white chest. The head is also banded, but with brown and white. The wings are long and pointed and show a broad, white stripe when the bird flies.

Habits: Killdeer are shorebirds but are often seen in dry meadows or ranchland. Most often ey will be found near areas of shallow water along the edges of streams. hey will run and feign a broken wing when their nest is approached.

Where to Look: The exposed flats of Oxbow Bend, Schwabacher Landing, d the meandering shores of the Snake River are good places to look.

potted Sandpiper

Family Scolopacidae, *Actitis macularius*

Description: In spring and summer, when the birds are most numerous here, this small shore-bird has distinct spots on its underside as well as its back. Spotted sandpipers are about six to seven inches long.

Habits: The spotted sandpiper walks along the shores of streams and lakes, bobbing its tail constantly. It will fly from place to place in a uttering, rapid wing beat with its wings curved downward.

Where to Look: The shores of the Snake River, mud flats of Oxbow Bend, d just about any small body of water in the park can be home to ese birds.

41

California Gull
Family Laridae, *Larus californic*

Description: This is a large "sea gull" that nests inland. The California gull has a white body and head, with a gray back and upper sides of its wings. It wing tips are black, and it has a red spot near the end of its bill.
Habits: Gulls are usually not far from water. In the park, they are attracted to areas where fishermen congregate, where there are boats and fishing activity, and wher they may scavenge from human activities.
Where to Look: Jackson Lake is ideal, especially around the developed mar nas of Colter Bay and Signal Mountain. These gulls can also be found mos times of day at the Jackson Lake Dam or the Oxbow Bend.

Osprey
Family Pandionidae, *Pandion haliaetu*

Description: These fish hawks are sometimes mistaken for bald eagles since both are large birds of prey, have long wingspans, and inhabi the waterways. The osprey is white below anc dark brown above with narrow wings that sweep back rather than point straight out.
Habits: Ospreys are most often seen circling above the water where they catch their prey of fish. These birds will hover over a fish then dive straigh down with their heads and feet entering the water together. They flap heavily out of the water, shake off in midair, and fly off with their fish.
Where to Look: Ospreys fish up and down the length of the Snake River and in most lakes and nest throughout the valley. Oxbow Bend and the Snake below Jackson Lake Dam are both good places to watch.

Great Gray Owl
Family Strigidae, *Strix nebulo:*

Description: This very large, mottled gray owl one of several owl species in the park. Nothin else is as big, except for the great horned owl, which has prominent horns on its head. The great gray owl's huge dished face and yellow eyes make it easy to identify.
Habits: Although it is uncommon, the great gra owl is often out in the daylight hours and is rela tively unafraid of people. It hunts for mice and voles in the morning and afternoon hours, in small meadows in the forest.
Where to Look: Great gray owls inhabit the pine forests along the base of the Tetons, so hiking the Valley Trail is a good option.

Broad-tailed Hummingbird   Trochilidae, *Selasphorus platycercus*

Description: Hummingbirds are unmistakable, with their tiny size, long slender bills, and rapid, insect-like wingbeats. Their wings move up and down at up to seventy beats per second and create a distinct humming or buzzing sound. The broad-tailed hummingbird is one of several species here in the park.

Habits: Hummingbirds feed on plant nectar and insects. They hover motionlessly in front of wildflowers and poke their thin bills into the blossom.

Where to Look: Oxbow Bend, around Jenny Lake, or at turnouts and trails along Cottonwood Creek are good sites. Look especially in mixed forests with wildflowers or where willows, water, and flowers are present.

Belted Kingfisher   Family Alcedinidae, *Megaceryle alcyon*

Description: This is a stout, gray and white small bird, a little bigger than a robin, with a large head and a big bill. It has an irregular crest sticking up on top of its head and a broad gray band across the chest.

Habits: The kingfisher seems to be either flying noisily up and down a stream, or sitting quietly on a branch above the water. From its perch, the kingfisher dives head first into the water to capture a small fish.

Where to Look: These birds prefer the quieter, calmer streams and shallow lakeshores where small fish can live. Jenny, Leigh, and String lakes are good sites, as well as side channels and tributaries of the Snake River.

Northern Flicker   Family Picidae, *Colaptes auratus*

Description: The flicker is a large brown woodpecker, about twelve inches from its head to the tip of its tail. It has a gray and brown head, with a black breast band. The male has a bright red streak between its cheek and throat.

Habits: There are several woodpecker species in the park, and all of them have similar habits. They have an undulating flight between trees, where they land on the trunk and prop themselves upright with their stiff tails. They chisel into the wood with their sharp bills to find insects.

Where to Look: Woodpeckers are in all of the park's forests, so a hike on any trail through the trees will be a good bet for seeing one of these species. Flickers and other woodpeckers often nest in hollow aspen trees.

Tree Swallow
Family Hirundinidae, *Tachycineta bicolor*

Description: Swallows are small birds with broad, pointed wings and square or notched tails. The tree swallow is white below and metallic blue-green above. The female is gray above. Other swallow species in the park are similar looking with slight variations in color and markings.

Habits: The three most abundant swallow species in the park can be identified by their habitats. Cliff swallows build colonies of dome-shaped mud nests under bridges and the eaves of buildings. Bank swallows nest in colonies in dirt banks, especially along the Snake River. Tree swallows nest in hollow trees.

Where to Look: Cliff swallows are common around the Snake River Bridge at Moose. Tree swallows can be found along the Taggart Lake Trail, and bank swallows are along the Snake River.

Common Raven
Family Corvidae, *Corvus corax*

Description: The common raven is all black from head to toe and has a wingspan of four feet. These large birds have long, shaggy throat feathers and a long, thick bill. Up close, the feathers can shine with an iridescent purple.

Habits: Ravens are superb fliers and can be mistaken for hawks at a distance. They have long pointed wings and can be seen soaring, diving, or doing aerobatics. They eat everything from carrion to berries, rob eggs from nests, catch mice, and scavenge from garbage cans.

Where to Look: Ravens are found throughout the park. Many of the scenic turnouts and picnic areas have ravens associated with them.

How to Tell Ravens and Crows Apart

Both the common raven and the American crow are found in the park, but ravens are larger and more numerous. Both species are all black. Crows have short, fan-shaped tails and less massive bills. Ravens have longer, spade-shaped tails. Crows' "caws" are higher pitched and more rapid than the raven's deep call. When crows first alight, they tend to flick their wings and tails.

lack-billed Magpie

Family Corvidae, *Pica hudsonia*

Description: Nothing else in the park looks like the magpie with its black head and back, white breast, and black and white wings. One unmistakable feature is the magpie's extremely long tail. Up close, the feathers shine with a green-black iridescence.

abits: Magpies hunt for insects and anything else they can find on the ound. They are efficient scavengers and are the first to find an elk or deer lled by the stresses of winter. Magpies build a ball-shaped stick nest, usuy in willows or other thick vegetation.

here to Look: Look for them around Menors Ferry, Blacktail Ponds verlook, Mormon Row, and Willow Flats Overlook.

ray Jay

Family Corvidae, *Perisoreus canadensis*

Description: This is an all gray bird, a bit larger than a robin. The back and wings are dark gray while the breast is a light gray. The beak and eyes are black.

Habits: These are forest dwelling birds and are extremely tame. They are commonly know as "camp robbers" for their habit of swooping into a camp and eating whatever food is left out.

here to Look: You can find these birds all along the base of the mounins, especially in the lodgepole pine forests near Jenny Lake, along the trail Leigh Lake, and around Taggart Lake.

teller's Jay

Family Corvidae, *Cyanocitta stelleri*

Description: The Steller's jay is somewhat similar to the blue jay, but heavier and with a long, black crest on its head. This jay is all blue with a black head and upper back. Adults have a few white marks on their foreheads.

Habits: Steller's jays prefer the coniferous forest mixed with a few other trees, and they eat seeds, fruit, and insects.

Where to Look: Any of the forested trails in the mountains can have a Steller's jay. Look on the trail to Paintbrush Canyon, Death Canyon, or Granite Canyon.

Clark's Nutcracker

Family Corvidae, *Nucifraga columbian*

Description: The nutcracker is a medium sized bird of the mountain forests, with a gray body a black wings. It has a short, black and white tail, white wing patches, and a straight, pointed bill.
Habits: Nutcrackers are usually seen flying fro tree to tree or perched in the top of a pine or fir. They eat mainly pine seeds, especially the high altitude whitebark pine.

Where to Look: Nutcrackers prefer coniferous forests, so look along the trails leading up into the mountains. The trail to Amphitheater and Surpris lakes will almost certainly have a Clark's nutcracker along the way or in th whitebark pines near the lake.

Mountain Chickadee

Family Paridae, *Poecile gambe*

Description: This is one of two species of chic adees in the park. They are almost identical except for a white stripe above the mountain chickadee's eye and a buffy color on its sides.
Habits: Chickadees are found in most of the park's forests. Their familiar "*chick-a-dee-dee*" ca is often easier to find than the birds themselves. They move constantly through the treetops.

Where to Look: Look for mountain chickadees in the pine and fir forests o the mountain slopes. Any of the trails leading up into the mountains will have them somewhere along the way.

American Dipper

Family Cinclidae, *Cinclus mexican*

Description: The dipper is a robin-sized bird wi a stubby tail and short wings. It is a uniform soc gray color, with pinkish legs and feet.
Habits: The dipper gets its name from its habi of dipping up and down as it perches on rock near a fast-moving stream. It jumps into the water and disappears to gather up aquatic inse in its bill. During nesting season, it returns to

mossy, ball-shaped nest to feed the young. Dippers are commonly seen flying up and down mountain streams and singing their songs.
Where to Look: In mountain canyons, the dipper is always found near rush ing water. They nest on cliffs or boulders near waterfalls. In the park, look for them along Cascade Creek on the way to Hidden Falls and in the strea between String Lake and Jenny Lake.

Mountain Bluebird

Family Turdidae, *Sialia currucoides*

Description: Males are a soft, brilliant blue, while females are bluish-gray with a gray breast. They are relatively tame birds and robin-like but smaller. Their call is a quiet little note.
Habits: Often seen perching on fence posts, tall weeds or shrubs, or highway markers, mountain bluebirds flutter gently down to catch insects on the ground. They usually nest in hollows in aspens and cottonwood trees.
Where to Look: Open meadows near aspen or cottonwood stands, sagebrush flats with stands of trees, or old hayfields are prime spots. Antelope Flats Road, Moose-Wilson Road before it enters the trees, and Lupine Meadows are good places to look.

American Robin

Family Turdidae, *Turdus migratorius*

Description: The robin has a gray back, dark head with white around the eye, and a rich, rusty orange breast. This is the same species found throughout the United States.
Habits: Robins are thrushes, with the habit of feeding on the ground for earthworms and insects. They nest low in trees or on buildings.
Where to Look: Robins can be found in most meadows in the park. The grassy meadows around Oxbow Bend, meadows surrounding Two Ocean Lake, or open areas along the Snake River are ideal.

Yellow Warbler

Family Parulidae, *Setophaga petechia*

Description: The male yellow warbler is bright yellow, and the female is a dull yellow, but there is nothing else that looks like them (The American goldfinch has black wings and tail.)
Habits: These little birds are most often seen flashing though willows and other shrubs and flitting about to catch insects on twigs and branches. Their nests are small cups woven into the upright branches of shrubs, often near water.
Where to Look: Yellow warblers are found all over the park in aspens, willows, alders, and other deciduous trees and shrubs. They are common around Oxbow Bend, Two Ocean Lake, Schwabacher Landing, and near Menors Ferry at Moose.

Western Tanager
Family Cardinalidae, *Piranga ludovicia*

Description: This medium-sized tanager looks almost tropical with its yellow body, red face and head, and black back and wings. The female is a duller yellow and has no red on its head.

Habits: Usually seen only in pairs or individually, western tanagers arrive in the area in large colorful flocks of hundreds of birds. Once on their nesting territories, they seem to disappear.

Where to Look: They like open forests, especially lodgepole pines on the moraines and flats near the Tetons. Look for them along the hiking trails not far from the trailheads, around Jenny Lake, and near Signal Mountain.

White-crowned Sparrow
Family Emberizidae, *Zonotrichia leucophr*

Description: This is a small, gray and brown sparrow with a distinct black and white striped head and a pinkish bill. The breast and belly are solid gray, and the wings and back are brown, black, and white.

Habits: The white-crowned sparrow prefers brushy places and sits up on top of low bushes to sing.

Where to Look: These sparrows live in the understory at the forest edge and in more open, brushy places. Look along any lakeshore, such as the trail to Leigh Lake, or in the sagebrush along the Antelope Flats Road.

Dark-eyed Junco
Family Emberizidae, *Junco hyemal*

Description: This is a small, relatively tame forest bird. Juncos are plump little birds with black heads, pink bills, rusty brown bodies, and whitish bellies. Females have gray heads. There are several variations of this bird.

Habits: This is a forest bird that prefers openings in the trees with brush and grass. They nest on the ground and are most often seen there or on low shrubs.

Where to Look: Try any of the park trails that wind through the forest. The Two Ocean Lake loop is good, as well as the west side of Jenny Lake or the trail into Paintbrush Canyon.

ellow-headed Blackbird Icteridae, *Xanthocephalus xanthocephalus*

Description: The male is unmistakable—a black bird with a yellow head and throat. It also has a distinct white wing patch in flight. The female is brown and somewhat smaller with only a hint of yellow on the front.

Habits: These birds live in the marshes and nest among the reeds and cattails. In spring and early summer, the males sit on tall reeds and sing their raucus songs.

Where to Look: Willow Flats, Oxbow Bend, and Christian Pond are good places to see blackbirds.

Western Meadowlark Family Icteridae, *Sturnella neglecta*

Description: Meadowlarks are roughly robin-sized, brown and white birds with yellow breasts and throats. There is a black band across the chests as well.

Habits: Meadowlarks live in open country and nest on the ground. They perch on fenceposts, sagebrush, and stalks of tall plants. When they fly, it is usually just above the vegetation, alternately flapping and gliding.

Where to Look: The eastern part of the park is ideal. Look anywhere along antelope Flats Road on sagebrush tips, or along Mormon Row on old nceposts. The males will be singing in May and June.

American Goldfinch Family Fringillidae, *Spinus tristis*

Description: Small, yellow birds that look almost like wild canaries, goldfinches are usually seen in small flocks. The male, with its bright yellow body, black wings and black-capped head, stands out much more than the pale yellow female. Both sexes have short, orangish, conical bills.

Habits: Goldfinches eat small seeds and tree buds. They prefer the seeds of many weed species, especially thistles. Goldfinches fly in an undulating pattern—alternately ising and dipping as they go—and often mingle with pines siskins.

Where to Look: These are birds of the open country, weedy fields, and adsides. Look for them in the old hayfields along Mormon Row, along antelope Flats Road, and in meadows near the base of the Tetons.

Fish, Snakes, and Amphibians

Jackson Hole has been famous for its fish since it was first settled in the late 1800s. Over the years, dude ranchers, tourists, and residents have caught the valley's fish for food, and old photographs attest to the number and size of their catches. The Snake River finespotted cutthroat trout, the only native trout, was a favorite. There are other trout species that were introduced over the years for sport fishermen, and there are fish species that have been introduced accidentally. Today, the trout in the park's streams and lakes are still a big attraction to visitors, and they support a number of professional fish guiding services within the park. However, with the increase of sport fishing and the travel between streams by fisherman with their gear, disease and parasites have made their way into the park. Loss of habitat, through the diversion of water for other uses or through drought, is the major cause of declining trout populations. The Snake River is controlled at Jackson Lake Dam, and the water is actually owned by farmers in Idaho.

Besides the larger fish, aquatic communities contain an array of other species—frogs, salamanders, snakes, toads, and minnows—that are vital to the ecology of the area. Some of these species are very susceptible to environmental changes, and their decline can indicate a widespread problem such as air pollution.

Three snakes, none of them venomous, are found in the park. The most abundant is the wandering garter snake. The other two are the valley garter snake and the rubber boa. The northern sagebrush lizard is the only lizard species found in the park, and it is rare.

Six species of frogs and toads occur in the park: Columbia spotted frogs, boreal chorus frogs, boreal toads, tiger salamanders, northern leopard frogs, and bullfrogs. The northern leopard frog, once common, may now be extinct. Bullfrogs were introduced and survive in some of the park's warmer waters.

Wandering Garter Snake   Family Colubridae, *Thamophus elegans*

Description: This is a small snake, usually around twenty to thirty inches long. It has an olive green to brown body with pale yellow stripes on the sides and back.

Habits and Habitat: Never far from water, the wandering garter snake is most common along the Snake River bottomlands.

Mountain Whitefish   Family Salmonidae, *Prosopium williamsoni*

Description: The whitefish is a silvery white fish common in the Snake River. It has a small, pointed mouth and larger scales than the trout. Whitefish can be mistaken for suckers but have an adipose fin (a small fin on their back between the tail and large dorsal fin) that suckers and chubs do not have.

Habits and Habitat: Whitefish live in the same waters as trout but are often found in schools, especially in the fall spawning season. They feed much the same way as trout, taking insects on the surface, as well as on the river bottom. The record whitefish caught in the Snake River weighed over four pounds.

Utah Chub   Family Cyprinidae, *Gila atraria*

Description: The chub is a brassy or silvery fish with a dark olive brown back. It is considered a "nuisance" fish by trout fishermen. They are small fish, but may grow to be over one pound.

Habits and Habitat: The Utah chub can be found in all park waters, but prefer slower moving water, backwaters, and sloughs.

Mountain Sucker   Family Catostomidae, *Catostomus platyrhynchus*

Description: The sucker has a dark green or dusky back with black specks, and a whitish underside. The mouth is large and downward-facing and can be wider than the head. Mountain suckers are found in cold, running water.

Habits and Habitat: They are abundant in the Snake River and grow to be several pounds.

Lake Trout

Family Salmonidae, *Salvelinus namaycus*

Description: Lake trout are a darkish green with white spots the full length of their body. They have a distinctly forked tail and often appear long and thin compared to other trout.

Habits and Habitat: These non-native trout were introduced as game fish and are well-established in the park. They move from top to bottom of the lake with changing water temperatures and are often near shore as the ice melts. Jackson Lake is full of lake trout. The state record was caught here from shore and weighed fifty pounds. They are also abundant in the Snake River just below Jackson Lake Dam.

Brook Trout

Family Salmonidae, *Salvelinus fontinal*

Description: A greenish silver trout, the brook trout has light spots on a dark background, including some red or pink spots with blue halos on the lower part of the body. Belly and tail are deep red and black with the lower fins and tail having a bright white border.

Habits and Habitat: Brook trout were introduced here as a game fish years ago. They are found mainly in smaller streams, beaver ponds, and lakes. The state record was over nine pounds.

Rainbow Trout

Family Salmonidae, *Onchorhynchus myki*

Description: A silver green trout with uniform black spots on its body and tail, the rainbow is named for a colorful band extending from cheek to tail.

Habits and Habitat: Rainbows are known for their strength and fight. They are found in low numbers in many of the park's streams. The Gros Ventre River is good rainbow habitat. Under ideal conditions they may reach twenty pounds, but not in these waters.

rown Trout

Family Salmonidae, *Salmo trutta*

Description: The brown trout looks somewhat like the brook trout, but has dark spots on a light background. It also has spots with blue halos. Unlike e cutthroat trout, the brown trout has no or few spots on its tail.

abits and Habitat: Brown trout are found in a number of park waterways d lakes. They are particularly concentrated in the northern end of the rk, in Jackson Lake and the upper Snake River that feeds into it. The te record, caught in a reservoir on the Green River, was over twenty- e pounds.

utthroat Trout

Family Salmonidae, *Onchorhynchus clarkii*

Description: A silvery greenish trout with black spots evenly distributed over its body, the Snake River finespotted cutthroat is

e of several distinct subspecies of cutthroats. (Other cutthroats have spots oncentrated toward the tail.) It has pinkish fins and tail and a pair of red ashes under its jaws. Older fish have a distinctly yellow belly. The state cord cutthroat (not a Snake River variety) is fifteen pounds.

abits and Habitat: Cutthroats prefer cold, clear, moving water, but can e found in most park lakes as well. They spawn in early summer in shallow reams and spring creeks that feed into their lakes and rivers. The Snake iver is the prime home of these beautiful trout. Look for them (but ou can't fish for them here!) in Cottonwood Creek by the Jenny Lake oat Dock.

WORK BY MICHELLE LAGORY. PRINTED WITH PERMISSION BY THE WYOMING GAME AND FISH DEPARTMENT.

Checklist of Common Wildlife

Mammals

Seldom Seen

Birds

Fish, Amphibians and Snakes

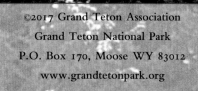

©2017 Grand Teton Association

Grand Teton National Park

P.O. Box 170, Moose WY 83012

www.grandtetonpark.org

Series Design by

Jeff Pollard Design & Associates
and
Ormsby & Thickstun Interpretive Design

Maps by

Mike Reagan

Project Coordinated by

Jan Lynch, Executive Director,
Grand Teton Association

Printed by

Paragon Press

ISBN 978-0-931895-67-8